BREAKFAST BOYS

SECOND HELPINGS

edited by Ian Frearson

*The line drawing on the cover
is by the late David Horobin.*

Copyright © Andrew Alexander, Charles Bristow, Neil Clarke,
Peter Dawson, Colin Dorman, Ian Frearson, Ray Hickling,
Geoff Hooley, Bill Millichip, Andy Moore, Robert Plant,
Ray Selby, Mick Shaw, Keith Smith 2021

Published by Peter Dawson
30 Elm Street
Borrowash
Derby, DE72 3HP

The right of Ian Frearson to be identified as the editor of this work
has been asserted by him in accordance with the Copyright, Designs
and Patents Act 1988.

British Library Cataloguing-in-Publication data
A catalogue record for this book is available from the British Library

ISBN 978-1-8383404-1-4

Printed and bound by Jellyfish Solutions Ltd

THE BOYS

Andrew Alexander
Charles Bristow
Neil Clarke
Peter Dawson
Colin Dorman
Ian Frearson
Ray Hickling
Geoff Hooley
Bill Millichip
Andy Moore
Robert Plant
Ray Selby
Mick Shaw
Keith Smith

CONTENTS

Contents

Contents

SMALL TALK

Ian Frearson

There comes a time in everyone's life when an opportunity presents itself that it seems cannot be denied. Three years ago some of the menfolk associated with Borrowash Methodist Chapel began meeting in a local café – Caffé Torta – to share breakfast. It soon became clear that the tales circulating round the tables merited a larger audience when one morning Peter Dawson, who we regard as our senior partner and mentor (largely due to his age), commented that he would love to have a tape recorder (told you he was old) on the table to record the stories, since many of them really merited being shared with others.

The gauntlet was thrown down and so it was decided we would write a book. Peter, an old hand at this and with his name already gracing the spine of many volumes, agreed to contact his publisher to see how they would feel about this and – more importantly and very generously – to fund its publication. What could we say? So, publication took place and the first of our books, Borrowash Breakfast Boys, was published in 2019.

Such was its success that we now have decided to repeat the process with a sequel – this small volume. So we come to the opportunity. If the book was to be done it needed a co-ordinator and more importantly an editor. That is why my name will appear in this volume as editor and why I feel it both a pleasure and a privilege to do it. Those who know Peter will understand that he is a hard act to follow. Those who do not, you have missed a rare treat.

When Jesus asked the various members of his close community to follow him they did so without question and in many cases in the middle of an already busy life. We do not have to make that sort of commitment but nevertheless it is testament to Peter, as both our spiritual and literary guide and encourager, that we maintain our interest and commitment to the book.

In 1812 Lord Byron rose and for the first time addressed the House of Lords. Part of his historic and memorable speech went as follows "I have traversed the seat of war in the peninsula; I have been in some of the most oppressed provinces of Turkey; but never, under the most despotic of infidel governments, did I behold such squalid wretchedness as I have seen since my return, in the very heart of a Christian country". He was not speaking of somewhere he had witnessed on his travels but here, England, the very land of his and ours.

In these troubled days of uncertainty and malady the future may look bleak but like so many before us we have our faith together with the company of friends around us to help overcome adversity and trouble. So we continue to live in hope that soon life may return to normal and we may once again recommence our forays into shared experiences.

Nothing is as easy as it appears it ought to be; so it has been with the production of this, our second volume of tales. Not all the original Breakfast Boys are still with us and we miss the stories the company and the companionship of those no longer here. It is a tribute to those that we now offer this slim offering of mixed tales for your delight, your education and your entertainment. Please do not be offended if I say, this book was not compiled for you but for us in order to remember each other and the combined companionship that has brought us and kept us together during the past three years.

So my personal thanks to Peter for his help advice and encouragement, to the boys for their continuing enjoyment of our breakfasts and to my wife Anne for her patience and dedication proof reading all the stories and accommodating my frequent and sporadic updates.

One of my maternal Aunts was a Doctor of Literature and retained a keen sense of humour until her death. Just before her 87th birthday I visited her. She asked what I would be buying for her forthcoming celebration. "A Book" I told her. She quickly responded "I already have one."

Good reading.

BORROWASH
Breakfast Boys

THE STORIES

SUMMER VACATION

Andrew Alexander

During one long summer university vacation I was able to travel to Israel and work as a volunteer in a kibbutz that was situated close to the river Jordan, which formed the boundary between Israel and the Country of Jordon. This was shortly after the 1960's war and tension along the border was high. The kibbutz itself was well fortified with armed guards, small gun emplacements and various ongoing patrols. We were well looked after and felt pretty safe.

It was very hot at the time and each morning we were driven down in the back of a lorry to the fertile fields accompanied by armed guards, who kept watch whilst we cultivated and picked water melons between 06.00 and 10.00am. After this it was deemed too hot to work so we withdrew up to the relative shelter of the kibbutz until late afternoon, following which we undertook another three hour stint. I made some good friends from different parts of the world on this trip and particularly remember the occasion when, soon after having been dropped off by the armed convoy to do our early morning session of work, a lorry came racing down the dirt track with lights flashing and horn blaring. "Drop everything and get in" the men in the back of the lorry shouted. We raced away back up the hill to the sound of gunfire from the hills above us.

When we reached the top we found a couple of field guns had been brought in by the Israeli army who were shelling a group of "insurgents" attempting to cross the border and approach the Kibbutz via the fields in which we volunteers were working. We were not allowed to stay and watch but had to return to the Kibbutz which was close by where we spent the rest of the day peacefully relaxing and later learned that the "insurgents" had been rounded up. All in the kibbutz were quite edgy after this but fortunately peace reigned.

After I finished my time at the Kibbutz I was able to travel around Israel visiting various cities/ towns and religious sites including Jerusalem, Nazareth, Bethlehem Caesarea, Sea of Galilee, Jericho and the Dead Sea. Not a good place to swim if you have a cut or a sore but OK if you want to float on your back and catch up with a bit of light reading. What a memorable and lively experience for a young impressionable university student in the late 1960s.

ALL RISE

Charles Bristow

It is the nineteen fifties. Bread is available in two alternative styles, fresh and stale. Summers seem to be sunny every day and last forever. Boys play cricket in cow pastures and seem to enjoy the additional hazards that come free with the location. Girls are admired from afar but remain an enigma. In the local courthouse the local Squire – (Roland Arthur Charles Palmer-Morewood) sits as chairman of the bench. He is a pillar of local society. A highly respected and totally unbiased foundation stone of the community. A man without any form of malice or prejudice. He dislikes everyone. This feeling with the parishioners of his little fiefdom is mutual.

He reigns supreme in the district as owner outright of a coal mine. The whole town is indebted to him and he knows it. He should do, it is his idea to remind the locals of it at regular intervals and he did, oh yes, he did. His mine, the Morewood's Colliery, is renowned for producing some wonderfully good quality coal – fit to power a steam locomotive. It is named "Swanwick Brights" after the seam that bore it. Tiny fossils of leaves and sea creatures are regularly found in the larger lumps as they are split open. It sparkles and glints in the sunlight. It is hard and burns hot with low ash content. But this is not what fascinates or occupies the Squire's mind at this moment.

He is a stout, non-athletic person whose idea of exercise is watching the hunt and standing quite still whilst others drive game towards his guns (beautifully matched Holland and Holland Sidelock ejector 12 bore shotguns – barrels bored improved cylinder and ¼ choke) over his head for him to frighten with repeated bangs and curses at the near misses. He is contemplating lunch – or more precisely, lack of it. His ever increasing rumbling tum reminding him that the hour for replenishment is past and soon his carefully prepared refreshment will be getting warm, after all he has earlier instructed that the cork be drawn at 12:30 sharp.

The case he is hearing is one concerning a miner who has allegedly stolen foodstuffs from the local Co-Op store in town. His town. The prosecuting solicitor is droning on about second offences and no mitigation for petty criminals of this sort. The ever present sun drives through the closed windows of the stuffy courtroom and adds to the existing fug of the day. The dust, lit by the sun's rays, rises and falls in a hypnotic dance in the still dry air, adding to the general stuffiness of the place. Around the court a motley collection of attendees droop visibly in the prickly heat of the public gallery, whilst on the Defence bench a florid and portly solicitor sits mopping his brow with a detached air of resignation. The Prosecution solicitor at last draws to a close, releasing his unwilling witness and prepares to return to his seat, at which the Chairman (the Squire) leans over towards him and asks the Clerk to the Court in his usual less than totally unbiased whisper "Are there any more witnesses on OUR side?"

EARLY DAYS

Geoff Hooley

I have always loved travelling by train. Let's face it, it is the civilised way to travel, after all unless you get a window seat whilst flying and it's a clear sky, all you can see is white cloud. We always went by train as we didn't have a car. Alright going by train takes longer but we make the journey part of the holiday experience. We've travelled on all sorts of trains, some pulled by steam locomotives, some, as in Belgium with graffiti on the sides, some where the angle of the chassis is about 30 degrees but the front and back are perpendicular for going up mountains and some, coming back through France, speeding along at 200mph.

At most large stations these days there will be a row of taxis waiting to whisk the weary traveller to their destination but that has not always been the case. I remember going to Scarborough on holiday one year. Waiting outside the station were Scarborough's young entrepreneurs with their pram trolleys waiting to take you and your luggage to your digs. I seem to vaguely remember that Dad haggled the price down from 10/- to half a crown. Ten bob was a lot of money in the late 1950s.[1]

Friar Gate station has been closed for many years, but I did travel from there once. We were going to Clacton and the direct train went from Friar Gate Station through Ilkeston, then on to Nottingham Victoria and down through East Anglia to Clacton. The only thing I can remember about the journey is passing over Nottingham's Midland Station which at the time I thought was a strange thing to do. I hadn't found out then that the British railways were originally made up of separate companies and the line we were on was run by the Great Northern Railway with the one below run by the Midland Railway.

Who introduced me to train spotting I can't remember but a lot of days during school holidays and Saturdays were spent at Spondon station waiting for trains. You always had to be down there in time for 'The Palatine' which came through at about 10:20 in the morning. This was a train which ran from Manchester to London every weekday. It did do the return journey in the afternoon around teatime but we'd usually gone home by then. A lasting memory of steam locomotives was walking

---

1   Ten Bob is pre decimal currency and is the equivalent to 50 new pence

along the tow path of the Derby canal as far as Chaddesden sidings one night. Lined up on the tracks were about 150 locos waiting to be broken up at Looms' yard. This was one of the many scrap yards up and down the country that had a contract to break up these wonderful workhorses when British Rail changed from steam to diesel.

Returning from holiday in Bournemouth one year I was fascinated when we got to the Lickey Hills near Bromsgrove. The incline of the track over a distance of 2 miles is the steepest in Britain and to get trains up it locos, known as bankers, were permanently on standby to give a helping hand by pushing from the back. Seeing a double header on the front of a train is one thing but seeing a double header on the back (which was needed this time) is another. The sheer power that was both required and available made one realise what can be achieved with water and a coal fire.

Once I graduated to owning a car train travel, because of the cost, was something that only happened very occasionally. That changed when we decided to go further afield for holidays.

CROSS HAIRS

Ian Frearson

It is a truth universally acknowledged by those who know him that Harry never was an academic. Both he and his brother excelled at solely one thing at school, disruption. They were loud and brash, incited or excited others into doing things they later regretted and generally made teachers speculate as to the burning reason that drove them to this juncture. They were in fact prime candidates for suspension or worse. Parental control was never a great element of their household and within the confines of their own restricted plot they caused havoc seemingly at every opportunity and with very little provocation. Their parents did encourage them to join various factions.

Cubs, then Scouts both came and went in short and quick succession, with nothing to show other than a letter from the leaders asking – or more correctly begging – that they keep their offspring at home where they could no longer disrupt the efforts of those trying to develop decent, likeable, useful residents from their children. It seemed that they enjoyed the ability to cause chaos from almost nothing, including stealing parts of uniforms, wrecking apparatus, bursting balls of various types, upsetting paint, breaking wooden display staffs and wresting trophies from their shields. In truth they seemed to be happy only when they were making everyone else around them miserable.

When Harry – the younger – attained the ripe young age of fourteen he was able to join the T.A. Suddenly his attitude changed. He seemed to have found something he actually enjoyed. Soon afterwards his elder brother joined him and together they formed a friendship hitherto unknown that quickly developed into a deeper relationship. They became smarter, more attentive, less rude and generally managed to keep appointments. Not only for the regular evening training sessions but others outside this small intimate society. They brought home trophies from training and competitions, especially it seemed since they both had very steady hands and now excelled in shooting. Mother silently prayed they would never be allowed to bring their rifles home.

Eventually the time came for them to face the dreaded Careers Officer interview at school, where even there they had made a positive impression on certain members of staff. This outside person, who it has to be said, thought of himself as the most important member of staff (even though he wasn't) walked around the school during his visits with a supercilious air of superiority, actions that caused deep resentment in the staff rooms and more than a little anger in some of the establishment. His idea of proffering helpful and useful advice was to speak to all pupils with equal disdain and in terms like "Forget anything useful boy, the best you can hope for is post office delivery or farm labourer". To girls, it usually ran something like "If you can manage to reach twenty without getting pregnant I suppose you could manage a factory job". His name was detested throughout the establishment and, it has to be admitted, many others as well. Fotherggil (possibly an assumed spelling by an equally obnoxious forebear) spat out his name like a Regimental Sergeant Major on a parade ground and everyone lay in hope for the day he met his Waterloo. Some, Harry included, made sure they did not have long to wait.

Pupils sat in three long rows outside the room more usually set aside as a common room, with faces and posture displaying no enthusiasm for what was to come. As far as Harry was concerned, he only had time for now so did not give a fig for the potential assistance that all knew would never come. Eventually pupils came and went so the line shuffled forward one seat at a time inching ever closer to an experience no one wanted but all had to face. Eventually one small mousey girl exited the room, in obvious distress, mopping tears from a long forlorn face with a small grubby tissue.

A loud voice bellowed out "Next" and Harry prized himself slowly and with inevitability from his seat. He swaggered his way into the room and immediately sat down. Fotherggil looked up, registered his disgust and barked "Who told you to sit?". "No one did so I did it" responded a voice that obviously carried some aggression. Fotherggil lost a little of his own attack and started shuffling through papers. Eventually starting off "I don't suppose for a minute that you have given any thought to what you might be when you leave…" He began, meaning to go on with some clever put down. Before he had a chance, Harry got in first with a rapid "Oh yes I have". Fotherggil was discombobulated, but had neither knowledge nor understanding to really appreciate what it meant. All he knew was that he loathed this young upstart who was clearly trying to better him. He would not allow it to happen.

"All right then, I don't suppose it will be anything that could be seen as useful but, you might as well tell me what your fertile mind and imagination has managed to drum up." Harry never took his eyes from Fotherggil as he responded, "I thought I might do something really useful for many people". He was clearly winding the Career's Officer up and Fotherggil was not a man to be treated like that,

"Come on then boy, come on, let's have it, just what do you think you would be capable of?". Harry looked him straight in the eye and, with two simple words, took the wind from his sails and colour from the hated official's cheeks as he calmly and quietly replied, "A Sniper".

ATTEMPTED HOROLOGY

Mick Shaw

I would have been around twelve at the time. My Uncle lived with us at this time and he had a really bright and shiny gold watch that had been a present from work some years earlier. It had stopped working and unbeknown to him I had decided to have a go at repairing it for him. During the course of this operation bits and bobs, springs and things sprouted all over the place. With no chance of making any further progress I packed most of the exploded parts back into the case and put it back where I found it, hoping no one would ever look at it again.

Some months passed and I had forgotten all about this episode. Well, my Uncle used to regularly take me to watch the Rams play football. On one Saturday as we made our way into town then on down Normanton Road towards the old Baseball Ground (via the pub) and on to the match, we suddenly turned into H Samuel the local jewellery shop. Suddenly my long forgotten memory returned with horror as Uncle took out the watch from his pocket and asked the assistant to take a look at it and assess the cost of repair.

As the back came off the watch all the loose bits fell out all over the place. The nonplussed assistant asked my uncle if he was having a laugh and pushed the whole mess back towards him. Once outside Uncle just gave me that certain look. Needless to say, it was a while before I returned into his good books, but I did learn not to try to mend watches.

NO SAFE HAVENS

Peter Dawson

The days of youth's adventures long ago
Seem hardly to have happened as they did.
How had he dared to risk his overthrow
In seeking to promote what he believed?

In dealing with life's challenges when young
We still press on when doubts fill us with fear,
Always seeming to be firm and strong
And know what we are doing, though not sure.

Men are not made for havens safe, so said
Mighty Aeschylus so long, long ago.
His words have echoed as the years have sped
Giving conviction that it must be so.

NO MORE PARAKEETS

Neil Clarke

Continuing my previous tales 'Parakeets on the Windowsill' recorded in the 'Borrowash Breakfast Boys' book, the 3 hrs flight from Sydney to Cairns is a bizarre one, moving from temperate city landscape to a tropical one, bordered by the Pacific Ocean.

Our apartment was owned by lady originally from Worcester, half way around the world yet close to our own home We dined early at a sea-front restaurant called 'The Raw Prawn' enjoying some delicious seafood, freshly caught but, luckily, cooked.

From this base we were able to undertake a number of exciting and different day trips, the first by train from Cairns to the 'Rainforeststation', high in the tropical rain forest. Here we had a photo opportunity to 'cuddle a koala' then continued travelling on an ex-army DUKW – an amphibious vehicle – to see another creature, the famed and feared saltwater croc. I never did get my swim that day. Later that afternoon, we took part in an aboriginal 'Dreamtime walk' with demonstrations of aboriginal hunting skills, Boomerang throwing and Spear throwing, followed by Didgeridoo playing. They then introduced the koalas, kangaroos and wombats.

From the Rainforeststation, back to Cairns was by Skyrail Cable Car, a system that was enormous. In places we were higher than the canopy, walking on wooden slats supported by steel cables. It was amazing. There were three places where you could climb even higher to enjoy the most amazing view, nothing but trees in every direction.

The entire system had been installed by Russian engineers, being the only ones at the time who were either daft or clever enough to position the enormous pylons which held the steel cables. Giant helicopters were used since there are no roads through the Barron Gorge. We walked along the raised boardwalks right up in the tree canopy. What a marvellous day.

Next day, we went on a completely different adventure, leaving Cairns harbour for the Great Barrier Reef. We joined a snorkelling and scuba diving group. Firstly, we had to fill out a questionnaire confirming that we were physically fit to go in the sea, only then were we kitted out in our wet suits ready for the snorkelling. As novices we attended a briefing on hand signals to be used to communicate with the boat when we were in the water. It was important for us all to stay together and we were split into groups of 3.

Flippers on and we safely fell off the back of the boat into the warm sea to join our guide. As we looked down, to get used to our equipment, it was really colourful with the coral and the fish (thankfully no sharks!). It was also, to my surprise, very deep. We were out for about an hour and it was not until our time was up that I realised just how far from the boat we had travelled, not because of how well we had swum, but because of the strong current. It was a struggle getting back on board which just showed us how exhausted we were.

Lunch was an amazing spread and when we had all eaten all we wanted, the crew tipped the remainder over the back of the boat to be consumed by the waiting fish. They were obviously used to eating the leftovers. For the afternoon, Jean got togged up to go scuba diving. So down she went, a bit deeper than in the morning, swimming with the fish. There was one big fat friendly fish, Wally, that was about 4-foot-long who let Jean pat him, as the instructor had indicated but nobody else would try it. We have a good photo of her holding up her hand as he paused for a photo shoot. All too soon we were back on board for the return journey to Cairns, about an hour. It appears all the houses in Cairns are built on stilts about 5 foot high, for the rainy season (we had hot rain every afternoon) and this also allows cooling air to flow under the house in the hot dry season.

The following day we toured the Flecker Botanical Gardens. There were many types of colourful plants, that we would consider in the UK as exotic. Also, many wild plants that grow in the area which have been used by the Aboriginals over a period of 40,000 years, as their major source of food, shelter, medicine, clothing, utensils, tools and weapons. At one time we could do all that. If only we could do it still.

As we walked around the area of Cairns, we noticed that the local river had warning signs telling you to take care as it contained freshwater crocodiles.

Leaving Cairns, the next day at 12.30, we travelled to Singapore via Darwin (for a fuelling stop), an 8-hr flight, arriving at Singapore at 6:30 pm. We stayed at the 'The New Otani' Hotel, next to Clarke Quay (no relation). The following morning, we had a walk around the area. The culture was definitely different to that of Australia. Local people were much more concerned with obeying 'the rules' for a start.

In the afternoon we went on a bus tour of Singapore, looking at all the main tourist attractions, including the large 'China town' and 'India town' as well as Raffles Hotel.

The following morning, we went on a tour of the Zoo, where monkeys and some other animals roamed free. The highlight for me was sitting down for breakfast with an orangutan and her baby. However, she didn't seem to want to share her breakfast with me! So, it was a jolly good job I had eaten before we left the hotel.

The fabulous spectacle of hundreds of different types and colours of Orchids that were growing, many just feeding on the moisture in the air, was absolutely fantastic.

On our last full day, we had the morning and afternoon free to explore. We used the Mass Transit Railway to get around, calling at Raffles for a 'Singapore Sling', as one does, then on to a nearby exhibition of Fabergé creations, returning to our hotel for a dip in the rooftop swimming pool. In the evening we had a tour of the harbour in a Chinese Junk 'Imperial Cheng Ho Ecru' as the sun set on a wonderful holiday.

Too soon our departure day came. We had a non-stop flight from Singapore to Heathrow which lasted 13½ hrs, flying over India and the Middle East.

A truly wonderful experience.

ASSISTED BURGLARY

Andrew Alexander

My professional career has been as a solicitor practising in Derby with the company I set up in 1977. By 1980 the practice had grown sufficiently to warrant moving from the original premises, comprising small rooms on the third floor of a property in The City Centre. So it was that, having acquired premises in a more desirable part of town, the time came for the move. To save on undue expenses, and in the tradition of all careful solicitors, we had decided to undertake the move ourselves. Dramatic scenes afoot.

All went smoothly until someone pointed out that the move would be obliged to include a substantial safe that was used for documents and money. This item was then situated on the top floor – a good start. A cunning plan was formulated whereby we would carefully "bump" the safe down three flights of stairs, gently load it onto a sack trolley and drag it up the road to the new premises. The first part we managed, namely "bumping" it down the stairs,

29

without major mishap. The second part, loading it was equally without spectacle, then three of us set off up the road taking turns about, with one pulling, one pushing and one resting. After some little time we became aware that we were the subject of much interest from the Saturday morning shoppers and passing general public, gazing on three men manhandling a heavy safe up the road.

It was about this time that we became aware of a police car siren and blue flashing lights racing up from behind. The car then dramatically screeched to a halt immediately in front of us. Out jumped a couple of sturdy officers who demanded to know what we were up to, as a report from a member of the general public had been received reporting a potential burglary of a safe by three men who were making away with it. A lengthy conversation with the officers then ensued before they accepted our explanation that we were acting lawfully, following which they helpfully and rather sportingly escorted us to the new offices, to the amusement of the many passers by. Thankfully and somewhat regretfully it is the only time I've had a police escort on my travels!

DON'T LET THEM
GRIND YOU DOWN

Charles Bristow
related to a breakfast companion

It had been one of those days when everything that could go wrong did, and when nothing else could go wrong, of course something did. It was almost as if the day had been written by John Steinbeck and, as such, did not disappoint.

Firstly, the appointment had not been met and the elder brother was driving home with less care than required or even demanded. He wondered about confiding in his younger brother Charles but dismissed the thought since he automatically thought it would result in criticism. His mind returned to his driving and the current situation. Not only did he not see the arrows, but upon interrogation by the police had admitted that he had "not even seen the Indians". They were less than amused and took full details. They explained that he had driven the wrong way up a one-way street. He carefully explained that he had only driven one way. They still appeared not to understand and in that matter of fact, official capacity way they sometimes have for making people feel unloved, reminded him that a summons was almost inevitable.

In due course he received the promised summons together with an offer that gave him, in lieu of an appearance in court, an opportunity to donate several tens of pounds by way of a fine, with an additional offer to achieve several stamps on his licence. He also received a photograph of the notices restricting access and other restrictions requirements and demands.

Being a sporting sort and enjoying the thrill of the chase, he duly sent a photograph of a cheque neatly made out for the required amount and with a note to say he hoped that this would suffice and see an end to the matter. Nothing was heard from them for some weeks, then, just as he thought the matter might actually be closed, he received a plain brown paper envelope with a familiar official stamp. Upon opening this he discovered that it contained nothing but a photograph of a pair of handcuffs. That day's return post saw him pay up in full.

LOSS

Ian Frearson

I lost another friend today, I did, I truly did.
How can it be that one so young should leave
　　　this World for me?
And yet he spent his last few days in more
　　　discomfort than was fair
But little said on how he suffered there.
I miss him and I wait with joy the day I see
　　　him once again.

I lost another friend today, I really truly did.
He spent his days in Arctic joy and trying hard
　　　with facial hair
But someone without one iota of that mind
　　　that shone so fair
In he who died under the wheels of selfishness
　　　and greed alone
Two thousand miles from his pure simple
　　　dreams.

I lost another friend today, yes that I really did.
He made himself a servant and a guide to
  those who came to say
I want to please with taste and smell and plate
  and glass alone today.
He brought it then astonished said you eat too
  fast to truly see
The love you could have had, no more until an
  hour has past.

I lost another friend today, I was expecting it,
  I was.
He joined with glee the tales of his and others
  set to please
And with his style and wit he set the tone to
  which we all aspired.
Then when the book was published made an
  impact with the pen and voice
I can't remember when I most enjoyed a meal
  so simple yet so good
In company alone it brought me everything I
  need so thank you one and all

I cried a cry of desperation Lord, so pure and
  oh so deep it was
That even I who heard it sighed and wondered
  if it could be true
That love of brother and of friend would ever
  mend when loss occurred

Loss

And thought that one just one last thought
    could bring me back to life
that one day Lord we would enjoy to hear each
    other laugh again.

COMPUTER SAYS NO

Geoff Hooley

We were going on a winter holiday to Bavaria and were to stay at Garmisch-Partenkirchen. These two towns were forced by the Nazi regime to combine as one, pending the winter Olympics of 1936. The journey to Brussels was uneventful. The journey from Brussels to Cologne was on the Thalys, a train designed to travel at high speed with all the latest bells and whistles. With its sleek lines and dark maroon paintwork it is truly an elegant sight when seen travelling from a distance.

The journey from Brussels goes via Liege, Aachen and then to Cologne. Liege-Guillemins station was at that time very impressive, with a tubular steel glass roof, five platforms (three of which are 450mtrs long) and nine tracks. At the time of our visit the station hadn't even been officially opened.

The stop was about 5mins, to disembark and embark passengers, then we pulled out to continue our journey, all ready for the speed rush. We passed over the river and had gone about a mile out of the station when the train stopped. There we sat talking amongst ourselves with nothing happening and daylight fading. After some little time we started to move but, hang on a minute, we were going back towards where we had just left. After a short distance we stopped again and started going forward (the driver had obviously realised we weren't going in the right direction) but our hopes faded once more when we stopped yet again, what was going on? The reverse journey started once more and this time we were almost back in Liege station before we stopped.

The next time we moved it was in a forward direction and to the parties' relief we kept going. The tour manager disappeared for a while and on his return he informed us that the computer had said 'NO'.

These trains are computer controlled and only trains like the Thalys are allowed to travel on the highspeed lines. For some reason the computer had got it into its little silicon brain that the Thalys was not a highspeed train and would not allow it to proceed onto the high speed line, even though the computer had been re-booted several times. So our journey continued on the normal lower speed line meaning that by the time we got to Cologne we were by then about two hours late.

The overnight stop was about an hour from Cologne by coach and on arrival at the hotel I think the staff were trying to blame us for the train being late and for them having to keep the kitchen staff on after 10 o'clock. Eating a hot meal at 11 o'clock at night though is not something to be recommended.

DEAD END

Ian Frearson

I enjoyed some little time last month listening, with some amusement, to a programme on BBC Radio 4, dedicated to the memory and work of Stanley Holloway. As programmes go it was pretty good. As entertainment went I considered it fantastic. During the course of the programme there were performance snatches from his various monologues, my favourite of which was "My Word, You do Look Queer". Of this, the lines I continue to love the most are "what age are you now? well 50, that's true. Your father died that age. Your mother did too." Believe me, the quality of the content is all in the delivery, timing of course being everything. It has become unfashionable to enjoy things of a bygone era, which is a great shame.

I can remember family parties, at which I was tolerated rather than encouraged, due to me being so much younger than all the other attendees. My mother being the youngest of five sisters, my cousins were all some years older than me, ranging from sixteen to twenty odd years, this made me a social pariah to them. In order to remain in the room and enjoy the party atmosphere I usually secreted myself into a corner, where I witnessed cousins playing 'Boogie-Woogie' music on a not too well tuned piano, and listened rapturously to scratchy 78's playing Ellington, Basie, Parker, Coltraine, Fitzgerald and even Crosby. Songs played, it seemed, mostly on black notes and with really amusing titles like 'Is Yo Is or Is Yo Ain't Ma Baby' and 'Bloop-Bleep' – this last still a firm favourite. So, it was with some sadness and regret that I recall the heady days of my pre-youth, due mainly to family matters that have recently overtaken other matters as an urgent priority.

My cousin died last week at the ripe old age of 96. This is somewhat poignant and more than a little circumstantial since, almost exactly one year ago, my mother died – also at the age of 96. As if this was not enough – although this one did occur many years ago (in fact when I was but a slip of a lad of 15) – my grandmother died at the age of 96. Now this may appear to be claiming a strangely impressive precedent for the whole family. This is not so. Admittedly, one Aunt did die at 97 but the remainder only managed a modest 85 or so. Still not too bad. Anyhow, be that as it may, on both the occasions of losing firstly my mother, sadly missed, and now cousin, undoubtedly to be missed, it has fallen to me to obtain & circulate the necessary formal paperwork required by so many 'Jobsworth' organisations which, for one good reason or another, find it impossible to accept ones word. By pure fluke, although with some real joy, it transpired that my cousin's doctor had also visited my mother.

He, a young athletic 38 year old, devastatingly good looking and with a real sense of humour (I hate him already) actually asked to see me when I went to collect her paperwork. I was pleased about this since it gave me the opportunity to thank him for looking after her so well. He smiled at this and said casually, "All I have done in the past eight years I have known her, was to administer a flu jab". I suppose at her age that is more than one could hope for. He also commented "You will notice that where it asks for cause of death, I have written 'Old Age'. She wasn't at all ill, she just wore out." Anyhow, having exchanged pleasantries about my mother, I had to repeat the process, one year later, about my cousin. He was equally kind & quick to explain that she too had just worn out, having suffered nothing more than chilblains during over half a century.

As I stood to shake his hand & leave, one small thought occurred to me. "I want to die at 96 years old," I began and he smiled. Then, just for effect, I added, "but I would much prefer to be shot by a jealous husband". He looked at me benignly and said, "dream on".

OUT OF THE FRYING PAN

Peter Dawson

After a successful teaching career, culminating in ten exciting but challenging years as headmaster of a purpose-built comprehensive for two thousand boys and girls in Greenwich, a restless spirit filled me. Might some new avenue of service await me? Not wanting to climb out of the frying pan into the fire, I asked my good friend Jesus for guidance.

Anticipating what my friend might have in store for me, I offered myself as a candidate for the Methodist Ministry. My devoted wife and I looked forward to circuit life, caring for the Lord's sheep in a group of churches.

It seemed that nothing would ever be able to compare with my ten years as headmaster of Eltham Green School, a typical Inner London comprehensive with enormous problems and opportunities.

Some of the young people were from criminal families. Interviewing the father of one boy who had been caught stealing, a man who was a prominent figure in the local criminal fraternity, he assured me that he was not going to let young Billy follow a life of crime. 'But', said I, 'Billy admires you and wants to be like you, and you're a crook, aren't you?' I was younger and braver in those days.

The man's minder, a huge character who stood with arms folded at the door, made to move forward but Billy's dad laughed and said, 'It's OK Joe. The headmaster's right.' Addressing me, he added, 'You see, I have a very high standard of living to maintain.' We parted on good terms, he assuring me that Billy would do no more stealing in school, and he never did.

Racial conflict simmered at the school, which had children of different ethnic origins. The white supremacist National Front had its London headquarters not far away. Black and white parents would confront one another at school functions. Long after my departure, Stephen Lawrence was murdered just up the road.

My somewhat forthright views having had a good deal of media coverage, I was a bit of a celebrity when I came before the district committee as a candidate for ordained Ministry. I learned afterwards that, most unusually, every member of the committee had turned up. I was not impressed. Some of their questions were pathetic and my feelings were made clear. A friend who was on the committee bumped into me next day and laughingly said, 'Peter, the committee was supposed to be interviewing you but some of them felt you were interviewing the committee.'

Happily, my candidature was successful so the way ahead seemed clear; but it wasn't! At this stage, the Lord who governs my life intervened. A telephone call from Derby – where on earth was Derby? – invited me to be interviewed for the post of General Secretary of the Professional Association of Teachers (PAT), a new trade union for teachers who wished to belong to an organization that would never, under any circumstances, ask them to go on strike. This was at a time when the big, militant teachers' unions had closed many schools in pursuit of pay demands.

Convinced that my friend Jesus must be behind this, I headed for Derby on what turned out to be a fateful Saturday. Arriving on the train from St Pancras, I was horrified to find the Derby platforms and concourse full of policemen. There were coppers on horses outside. What kind of a place had I come to? It turned out that Derby County were playing Stoke City in the FA Cup.

As a couple of escaped Londoners, we came to love Derby and its welcoming folk, who were known as 'meducks'. But my new job was no less demanding than running a school had been. The teachers' union I had been appointed to lead was involved in education politics at a time when confrontation with government and local education authorities was the name of the game as far as the other unions were concerned. They saw me as a pariah in arguing for the force of argument rather than the argument of force.

But, at the outset, my biggest problem was what to do about my entering the Methodist Ministry. It was resolved for me by the bright and shining ones at Methodist HQ. They placed me on a ministerial training course at Nottingham University with a view to my remaining as leader of the Professional Association of Teachers while training and staying in that post after ordination. The top gun at the Methodist Division of Ministries said: 'We don't have a Minister running a trade union and it will be good to have one.' I was to be what was called a Sector Minister, earning my living in a secular occupation while promoting my Ministry there and in nearby churches.

So it was goodbye to dreams of being a circuit Minister and hullo to the maelstrom of politics. In my prayers I told my friend Jesus: 'Here's another fine mess you're getting me into. I hope you know what you're doing.' He did, of course. He always does. I headed for the political jungle, not sure what I was getting into. I imagined that Christopher Columbus must have felt the same as he climbed aboard his ship and sailed westwards, hoping not to fall off the edge of the world.

A NEW HOPE
The Three Dimensions
of a Complete Life

Rob Plant

We asked our three year old son what he wanted for Christmas. 'Doctor gloves' and 'spidey web shooters' were top of the list, followed by a fireman truck: All the tools of his current favourite role models.

To a young mind, with a playful imagination, everything is immediately possible; then, as we move through the trials of life, the mental equipment of 'grit' and 'hupomone' can prove necessary, underpinned by love as a source of power.

In 'A Defence of Prejudice: And Other Essays', 1911, John Grier Hibben wrote: 'Not only is progress assured by overcoming resistance, but resistance itself is an essential factor in progress. No leverage is possible without the resisting medium of a fulcrum; so that without resistance it would be impossible for us to get a foothold upon the earth even in the ordinary act of walking. We know that it is not only the strength of the arm, but the stubborn stuff of the bow which speeds the arrow. Moreover, a current of electricity, passing freely through its conducting wire, gives no visible evidence of its existence; but when it meets the resistance of the carbon points, it bursts into light. In the world of human affairs and relations, much of the light has its source in the clash of opposing forces, and the struggle to overcome resistance.'

What then, when encountering resistance, should we consider at each fork in the road of life; do we take a path of meaning or one of expediency?

Martin Luther King Jr. framed the three dimensions of life as length (the inward concern for one's own welfare, that causes one to push forward, to achieve personal goals and ambitions), breadth (the outward concern for the welfare of others) and height (the upward reach for God) and he made the following observation:

'In a sense every day is judgment day, and we, through our deeds and words, our silence and speech, are constantly writing in the Book of Life.

Light has come into the world, and every man must decide whether he will walk in the light of creative altruism or the darkness of destructive selfishness. This is the judgment. Life's most persistent and urgent question is, "What are you doing for others?"'

Throughout life, there's always something we can learn from our role models.

LAS VEGAS OR BUST

Andrew Alexander

During the 1980s, my wife Helen and I made a trip to North America. This included a visit to Las Vegas and then on to San Francisco. We were not by any means going to be too early for our flight when we duly checked out of our motel and took a taxi for the twenty-minute ride to the airport. By the time we got through to the check in desk the final part of check in was underway and our conversation went something like, "Pass me the tickets" – me to Helen. Back came the urgent response "You've already got them". Me again – "No I haven't". Ugh Ugh as I realised the last time I had seen them was at the motel check out. We could be in for a bad time here.

In the days when there were no mobile phones or easy online means of contact, I needed to take some action. Fast. I opted to leave Helen at the airport with our luggage and, having raced to the airport entrance, wisely chose the slowest taxi that had ever been hired. The driver just wanted to chat and didn't seem to understand that I needed him to break all speed limits. When we finally got back to the motel, I dashed into the reception and started wildly hunting about, until another guest, seated at a low table, shouted, "Are you looking for these?" There were the tickets lying smugly and safely on the table. Back then into the waiting taxi who proceeded to drive like it was a horse and cart despite all attempts to whip him along!

Finally back at the airport I joined an agitated Helen and we raced to the gate number shown on the departure board. Of course only then did we discover that the gate had been changed, with the revised one helpfully located at the other end of the airport. The plane was due to leave at that moment but we dashed to the revised gate and were met by staff who ushered us down the corridor towards the plane with a smile and reassuring shouts of "if they're closing the door you've had it". They were closing the door but a cheerful young hostess yelled out "Jump in we're off". We did and as we made our way to our seats I looked out to see the plane already reversing out to make its way to the runway. Phew! And my marriage was still intact.

Still, it happens to us all doesn't it?

WAR CHILDREN

Ian Frearson

There are fewer of us now than hitherto purely due to the Scythe of Time himself and his determination to manage the World's population in the only way he knows. However, there was a time when war babies were a common and dominating feature of the population. I am one of those many and varied people who was conceived in the times of great crisis and uncertainty when life expectancy was limited, in a great part, by luck.

Sitting in the cold and unrelenting discomfort of a Normandy trench was a group of Notts & Derby Sherwood Foresters Infantry. Try as they might the awful situation and suffering they were going through had not yet dampened their spirits to the point where they could not enjoy a little light relief. One or two were opening parcels and packages recently received from home, others were trying hard to disguise a tearful visage as they read and re-read passages of letters from loved ones safely (they hoped) at home in blighty.

One old veteran, a local yokel – a rough diamond from the mining area of Derbyshire – sat contemplating his missive with a stern face showing no emotion until, with a shout and a laugh, he announced to all who were within hearing distance "Hey lads, I'm going to be a father again". The trench and all its occupants went strangely and suddenly silent. The reader looked round with some mixture of disbelief, suspicion and lack of understanding. "What's the matter with you lot" he went on, "I think that is something to celebrate, my wife and I were trying for another baby well before I was sent over here and now we are having one".

One of the less simply educated companions took a little pity on him as some of the others sniggered and attempted to look away so he tried to make the simple facts more clear. "Yes, but you been over here quite a while now George" he stated. "What has that got to do with it then?" asked the still confused receiver of glad tidings. "Well we have been together here now three years next month so don't you think that is a little strange that your wife should become pregnant after all this time?" came the suggestion from the potentially helpful companion. "That's nothing," rang out the final and defining comment "I still don't see what that has to do with it, there are seven years between me and my brother."

INTO THE FIRE

Peter Dawson

Twelve years of fighting the good fight of Christian witness in the jungle of education politics took its toll. On my retirement at the end of it my wife and I went to a weekend of Christian fellowship. In a passage of scripture to which a speaker referred, my eyes fell on these words of the prophet Joel: 'I will restore to you the years that the locust has eaten.' My heart was strangely warmed.

Not all the hostility towards me in my role as a trade union leader in the world of education politics came from the big unions that favoured disruption to debate. My public pronouncements, newspaper articles and appearances on radio and television upset the Methodist establishment, whose politics are left of centre while mine are right of centre.

One circuit Minister initiated proceedings to have me disciplined and unfrocked. In a speech to the annual conference of the Association, I had drawn attention to the problems schools faced as a result of the growth of the single-parent family.

I was attacked for scapegoating girls struggling to raise children on their own.

It was my practice regularly to visit our federations and discuss with teachers their current joys and sorrows. Increasingly, I was told that members were faced with children being brought up by young girls abandoned after getting pregnant. They struggled with the demands of parenthood and their children came to school unable to dress themselves, ignorant of the alphabet and wildly undisciplined. 'These days', said one primary school teacher with many years of experience, 'we are more like social workers than teachers, having to make up for problems at home with the collapse of the family with two parents.'

A distinguished Oxford sociologist had asserted that young people brought up in single-parent situations were less likely than others to succeed at school and more likely to end up unemployed and to get into trouble with the law. Clearly, teachers' concerns were justified. But my drawing attention to this caused media uproar. My speech made the front pages of five national dailies.

He who advocated disciplinary proceedings against me was quickly silenced when he discovered that I would welcome the move. It would give me an opportunity to publicize the case for the church's teaching on marriage at the time, and to challenge the emerging alternatives.

In the world of education politics, I was careful not to broadcast my status as a Methodist Minister. Best let people discover it for themselves and make of it what they would. Amazingly, individuals who had locked horns with me all day during pay bargaining would come to me surreptitiously afterwards for advice on personal problems.

The first time it happened, I had to hide my surprise. 'Peter,' said a leading member of one delegation, 'I understand you are a Methodist Minister. My parents are Methodists and I was baptized in a Methodist Church as a baby. Might I share a personal problem with you?' It turned out that the man had been unfaithful to his wife. He wanted to tell her before she found out and ask her forgiveness. How should he set about that?

My twelve years in the political jungle brought me into close contact with whoever happened to be Secretary of State for Education in the government. The most extraordinary of them was Keith Joseph. He did not get on with his civil servants and liked to go his own way.

One day, he rang me up and asked me to meet him in his office next morning at eight o'clock. I duly took an early train to St Pancras next day and presented myself at Sir Keith's office at the Education Department. His civil servants had not yet arrived. He made us coffee and said, 'Truancy. I've been thinking about truancy.' You had to be careful when Sir Keith had been thinking about something. He had some odd ideas.

'There's too much of it, isn't there?' he asserted. I agreed that truancy was a problem but pointed out that some teachers preferred it if some pupils were absent. 'Good heavens', he replied, 'why would that be so?' I explained that the presence of a highly disruptive pupil in a class could make teaching impossible. Persistent truants were almost always dedicated to disruption if and when they attended.

But Sir Keith was determined to reduce truancy. He had worked out what to do. If a pupil was missing from a lesson, the teacher should immediately go out of school and fetch him. He should go to the truant's house, knock on the door and tell the parents that, unless they got young Jimmy into school, he would do no better than they have done. I winced at the thought of the reception some teachers might get, which might not fall short of physical assault.

I pointed out that we already had education welfare officers (EWOs) whose duties including pursuing school truants. They were trained to make clear to parents the legal consequences of failing to get their children into school. The man in charge of education had never heard of them.

While conducting my ministry in the secular world, I was often asked to look after a church that was for some reason without a Minister. That usually began with the Chairman of the Methodist District ringing me up and asking if he could pop in for a cup of tea. I also preached by invitation in all sorts of places. On one memorable occasion, I was invited to preach at Norwich Cathedral on Education Sunday.

It was parish communion and the Cathedral was packed to the rafters. Long-retired Anglican clergy had been brought in to administer the sacrament at different points. The Bishop had given a dispensation that, although only a Methodist Minister – how low was the Church of England prepared to go? – I might be allowed to help distribute the eucharistic elements.

I was introduced to a very kindly clergyman who looked so old that he might have known Adam in the Garden of Eden. He said, 'Peter, you take the chalice and I'll give the wafers, and stick close to me at all times. I say that not because I think a Methodist doesn't know how to administer the sacrament but, at any time, I might fall over.'

Although life was sometimes a bit frantic, there was an enormous benefit in leading a trade union and caring for a church at the same time. Each area of activity enriched the other. My secular occupation supplied my preaching with abundant evidence of the Gospel at work in the every-day world; my church provided a steady foundation for my faith in what were often godless situations.

In a publication entitled 'Holy Orders in Unholy Places', I explored the implications of sector ministry. Perhaps the time might come when all Ministers would earn their living in a secular occupation and conduct a church ministry of some kind at the same time. I would recommend it.

LONG ARM OF THE LAW

Charles Bristow
related to a friend and breakfast companion

It was not unusual for Charles to be taken to town by his mother for their weekly shop, in fact, it was the norm. Whilst it posed to him a number of restrictions by removing his opportunity to play with the gang, it frequently managed to offer more of an entertainment than a chore. So it was that one cold grey Saturday morning, that he remembered with delight, was dominated by an event that provided him with a party tale, on which he dined not only frequently but long into manhood.

The two of them (Charles and Mother) had taken the local service bus into town, then walked along towards the top of Normanton Road and turned into Sacheveral Street. As they did a sight met them that from that moment on was indelibly etched into both their memories.

In the middle of the road a burly police constable was trying vainly to drag an huge bundle towards Wilmot Street. As Charles and mother grew closer the bundle turned out to be a horse. The poor creature had, it appeared, dropped dead in the process of undertaking its daily duty between the shafts, but the reason for the current situation was not apparent until mother made her enquiry.

Although the policeman was obviously some years her senior she spoke with some considered respect. "Young man" she began, "What do you think you are doing?" He responded with some difficulty, red faced, gasping and panting as he laboured for breath "Well. Missis, (puff), I'm tryin' (pant) to get this 'ere (gasp) creeture (Puff) round inter Wilmot (puff) Street ready fer my report Missis". Now to some people this may well have been an adequate response detailing his justification but not mother. Mother needed more and responded that she could see what was happening but required to know just why. The red faced and sweating officer stopped his struggle, stood up and mopped his face with a large handkerchief. He then looked at mother. Rather shame facedly he then admitted "Well missis, yer see it's like this, I can't spell Sacheveral".

THE AQUARIUM

Geoff Hooley

Up until around 2000 we'd always taken holidays as a family in England but we decided it was time we went further afield. Our first foray into Europe was a long weekend trip to Belgium by coach.

As with all coach holidays there were several pickups on the way down to Folkestone where four coaches gathered before crossing via the Euro Tunnel. Two coaches were heading for Paris and two for Belgium. On arrival at the Euro Tunnel terminal and booking in the passengers were swopped onto the right coach for their destination ready for the crossing.

Off we went to our various hotels and had a wonderful weekend before gathering at the Calais terminal for the return journey. All passengers returned to the coach that had originally picked them up and we were set for the crossing.

When crossing the Channel through the tunnel on a coach they advise that if you suffer from sea-sickness it is better to get out of the coach whilst in the tunnel. The reason for this is that the contra-motion rocking of the train and coach can make it feel like a rough sea. That apart it's nice to stretch your legs before a long journey.

In each carriage there are a couple of very small windows which really only let you know when you've entered or left the tunnel. I was standing alongside one of these when a man from our coach came alongside me and looked out to see what he could see. After a short while the conversation went something like:

Man: Where are we?
Me: We're in a tunnel crossing under the
        English Channel.
Man: What's the English Channel?
Me: It's a 22 mile stretch of water between
        France and England

Man thinks about this before continuing

Man: Will we see any fish?

It turned out he was from the middle east and was on holiday with his girlfriend, trying to see as many places as he could before returning home.

I never did find out if he really understood about the Chunnel.

SOMETHING ELSE

Ian Frearson

It was approaching our wedding day. At the time we were both impecunious parties so had little to spend on fripperies and the like. Nevertheless, I had promised my lovely wife to be a honeymoon she would not forget and being a man trying to be a man of my word I was there to see that I delivered and that she was not disappointed. I mulled over all the alternatives, including the month in Madeira that we had lost the year before, due to me being called as an expert witness in a court case. May I add right now that this never actually happened, and I had felt aggrieved about it ever since, so did consider it. No chance of affording anything like that at our stage in the proceedings so a reconsider was required.

How about some time in Scotland, after all, she had lived in Edinburgh for a substantial period of her life? Wonderful scenery, good climbing – no, somehow that would not quite fit the bill either. I was aware that she had come from a City background so was unused to the rigours of the countryside and all it entailed, so had to reduce my options. I know, I thought rather stupidly, a cruise, but where to? Caribbean? No chance, far too expensive. Mediterranean? Nope, still too expensive – and in any case, as far as I knew she may not yet have a passport. Scandinavia? You must be joking, even a glass of water was out of my budget there. Radical thinking required.

Right, let's start again. A few days in a nice hotel in the Lake District? Not a bad idea since, after all, if there was nothing else to do there was always some good climbing. Drop that thought right now stupid man. Ok then, how about some time on the South coast? Not bad, but it was the wrong time of year to go topless on the beach, and in any case, I did not indulge in that very often since the sun does not like me and I always burn. Not in early March though surely? Right, I thought, let's get down to it seriously. Make a note of all the considerations and cross off the ones that are unsuitable or out of my league. I did, it worked. When people asked me, "what did you do for your honeymoon then?" I have no hesitation in telling them that I gave Anne the full range from which to choose.

I actually listed all the places I had considered, whether or not we could realistically have afforded to go or not, cruises, exotic places, hot countries, beautiful countries, mountain regions, seaside, lovely hotels, themed holidays, dangerous countries, cold countries, World famous landmarks, relaxing holidays, food orientated, sport orientated, people orientated and lastly a simple break locally. I asked her to make her choice and waited for the outcome with all fingers crossed that she would not choose one that would leave me destitute for the next twenty years. Finally, she looked at me with her devastating smile and I knew she would choose wisely, then she simply said, "I want something else".

In the end I plumped for three day's camping in the snow at the head of the Winnats Pass. Perfect, just perfect. One day she will acknowledge it and thank me for it.

BAD SCHOOL DAY

Mick Shaw

One snowy Winter's day, me and my school mates thought it would be a good idea to snowball the Ticknall Kids waiting for their bus to arrive in Melbourne market place. Unfortunately I had not spotted the Headmaster waiting as well and managed to send a direct hit into his earhole. His reaction was as expected "Shaw, I will see you first thing Monday morning in assembly". With this happening on Friday it gave me the weekend to plan my excuse for skipping school Monday.

When Monday came round I was really physically sick with worry and managed to con a full week off school. I imagined that, having missed a full week, Wild Bill (our nickname for the Headmaster) would have completely forgotten about the whole affair. Imagine then my horror at his first words in assembly the following Monday morning as he rasped out "Shaw, out here boy". Now Wild Bill was not called that for nothing as he did love to dish out the punishment. I stood in front of the whole school with my hand held out ready to receive the cane. At the first stroke I pulled my hand away causing him to miss me completely, lose his balance and fall over in the process. The whole school erupted into laughter and I thought 'this is not a good situation'. He doubled his efforts and I received three of the best on each hand. He was fully airborn on each successive delivery with his spectacles flying off in the process, his hair horizontal and quite literally foaming at the mouth as he uttered "Did you really think that I would forget lad? Well think again boy.".

My day did not get any better. My hands swelled up really badly and I could not hold a pen properly to do any work, resulting in receiving detention. Once back at home for tea I could hardly hold my knife and fork to eat with. My dad noticed this and made me show him my hands and explain their condition. "Had the cane lad? Been up to no good?". Off came his thick leather belt and I received six more of the best, this time on my backside. His parting comment as I was sent prematurely to bed "That might teach you to get the cane lad." Needless to say I was on my best behaviour for a while. But not forever.

QUICK QUOTES

Peter Dawson

"My mind to me a kingdom is."
William Wordsworth

"Give me a child until he is seven and I will show you the man."
The belief of the Jesuits about shaping a child during his upbringing to believe in Jesus.

"A woman is only a woman but a good cigar is a smoke."
Attributed to Winston Churchill among others.

"If you think nobody cares about you, try going overdrawn at the bank."
Anon

"Courtship is that period during which a girl decides whether she can do any better."

Billy Graham

"When I use a word, it means whatever I choose it to mean."

Humpty Dumpty

"I don't always know what I'm talking about, but I know I'm right."

Mohammad Ali

"You are not to keep company with men. You may not loiter in ice cream stores. You may under no circumstances dye your hair. Your dresses may be no shorter than two inches above the ankle."

Rules for school mistresses at a school in New Zealand in the nineteenth century.

"When in doubt, stick your left out."

Henry Cooper

"The only place success comes before work is in the dictionary."

Vidal Sasoon

Quick Quotes

"When I go to hear a preacher in his pulpit, I like him to appear to be fighting bees."

Abraham Lincoln

"Anyone who enjoys being in the House of Commons needs psychiatric help."

Ken Livingstone

"Church is like a swimming pool. All the noise is at the shallow end."

Andrew Marr

WAITING FOR GODOT

Charles Bristow
related to a breakfast companion

I remember well the heady days of single glazing and squeaking doors with mixed nostalgia. For some years we lived in a Police house, thanks directly to my father's occupation as local bobby. One of the built in features was the addition of two individual cells, attached to the house and accessed through the kitchen. Apart from this the house was singularly unspectacular and comprised the usual kitchen, dining room, front room, three bedrooms, a small sparse bathroom and a toilet conveniently situated at the bottom of the garden.

In Summer this was a haven for flies and their nemesis, spiders. In Winter it represented a challenge and a place of severe discomfort, being freezing cold. So cold that a small paraffin fuelled lamp (the Tilley) was permanently introduced throughout the nights, not for human comfort but to reduce the chance of burst pipes through the threat of them freezing up completely. These were the days of proper winters, when birds were known to die of cold whilst on the wing seeking out the very food that might prevent their final act, and young boys suffered the permanent ring of discomfort caused by the combination of short trousers, sliding socks and the tops of wellington boots on tender young skin – chapped legs.

It occurred to me one day during a very cold and uncomfortable contemplation that there was something not quite right about our current situation. You see, the arrangements of the house were such that humanity played a large part in its planning in that the cells had their own boiler and more importantly to prospective occupants, each one had its own W.C. Inside of course.

Now to a young man of enquiring mind and some ingenuity this seemed like unfair treatment to the family. Why, I considered, should miscreants and ne'r do wells enjoy the benefits and luxury of indoor plumbing whilst those employed to remove them from society did not? Admittedly the residents did have a better seat but apart from that the situation appeared to a young mind simply to be inequitable.

Well one day I decided that what was good for the poacher was good for the gamekeeper. Father was out on his rounds 'evenin' all' and all that, Mother was out shopping. As the call of nature slowly became both more apparent and acute I decided that common sense had to prevail and the facilities so well provided ought to be called into action more often. I headed into one of the cells and towards the inviting presence of the heated toilet.

Halfway through the event I suddenly had an alarming thought. What if there was an ominous clunk as the weighted door of the cell, so wonderfully designed to operate independently of human effort, clanged shut. I immediately required the services of the toilet more urgently than previously thought. Having made good and long use of the facility, I then began to consider the situation. The keys to the cells were kept just out of sight in the Kitchen. Tantalisingly close to the cell doors but obviously far from the arms length reach of a small boy. There would be no alternative but to sit it out and await the return of one parent or other. Praying alternatively that it would be first one then the other, imagining the repercussions from either.

It would feel like waiting for Godot.

TRIP TRIP TRIP TO THE LOO

Ian Frearson

A telephone call from head office to site requested that at least one site engineer was required to go and assist at the new harbour works in Greenock. The short straw fell to me. So along with my faithful assistant I set off. The journey from Derby to Glasgow was much longer in those days (at least it seemed that way) so we did not arrive until tea time. It was far too late to start anything on site that day so we repaired to the room we were to share.

As was the custom in those days, digs had already been secured by the firm and so we found ourselves reluctant refugees in a doss house with little but the road out of town to recommend it. It transpired the landlady, known to us as Mad Morag, who was a thin, pale, emaciated, chain smoking woman of an uncertain age, hated everyone who was not Scottish. The food was not the best (but it was consistently close to the worst). Meals repeated themselves with alarming regularity both in frequency of appearance and digestion. The beds were lumpy and noisy, the sheets thin the blankets itchy and the rooms smelled faintly of a Hammer House of Horror film set.

Perhaps the least attractive feature was the toilet paper, that was always IZAL brand. Sandpaper rough on one side, shiny and skiddy on the other. My companion hated it but, along with me I have to admit, was too scared to complain. In fact, he loathed it so much that he frequently took matters into his own hands to avoid having to use it. In order to undertake this expedition without mad Morag knowing, he sometimes left the house during breakfast to visit the public toilets. These were located some three minutes walk down the road. On one fateful occasion he was rumbled as Morag the Mare (as we also called her), spotted his surreptitious return.

"Where in God's name have ye bin laddie?" she spat out, two inches of ash falling from her cigarette, thankfully clear of the breakfast tray. Michael was clearly phased but put up a determined resistance with his response. "Well if you really want to know, I have been to the toilets on Argyle Street." Morag was obviously a religious person and immediately retorted "In God's name why – do we not have a perfectly good toilet here?" Michael had by now begun to warm to his task and responded with with a cool "Yes but there is no toilet paper in the loo here again". Morag was clearly aghast at being spoken to like this and shouted out "Do you not have a tongue in yer heed?" Michael's response closed the conversation and removed all doubt about his ability to stand up for himself.

He drew himself up to his full height and in a cool but determined voice said "Yes, but I don't have a neck like a giraffe".

ONE FOR THE GIRLS

Peter Dawson

Jimmy Barton, seventeen, did not like girls. They laughed at him at school. Well, he was a bit of a weed. Short and skinny, with a squeaky sort of voice, he knew he didn't amount to much beside his confident contemporaries like Bill Soames, captain of rugby. His easy manner and casual sense of humour had the girls hanging round him with a sparkle in their eyes. Nobody sparkled round Jimmy.

At seventeen, with the raging power of puberty making sexual attraction important for a chap, Jimmy knew he was a no-hoper. Little did he know that his outstanding cleverness, of which he made no fuss, had Suzie Wilson swooning over him.

'Oh come on' said Janey Butler, she of the bulging bust, big mouth and not much brains, chatting in the lunch hour about the boys, 'Barton's an utter wimp.' 'Well I like him', declared Suzie, 'he doesn't think he's God's gift to the human race like that Bill Soames and his mates.' She added, with great conviction: 'Most boys are so arrogant. And they've only got one thing in mind when they look us up and down.' 'That's what I like about them', said Janey, with a deep laugh.

Jimmy was always generous to any sixth former doing A Level physics who was struggling with a problem. His ability to make the solution easy to understand was a gift that would one day make him and excellent teacher.

When it was announced in school assembly a year later that James Barton had won an open scholarship to Cambridge to study physics the applause was resounding, although there were many in the upper sixth unaware of the identity of who they were clapping. Not, of course, Suzie Wilson, who sought Jimmy after assembly to congratulate him. Throwing her arms around him, she kissed him warmly on the cheek and declared, 'Well done, my hero.' An astonished Janey Butler, who witnessed this, told Jimmy, in mischievous mood, 'Our Suzie does that to all the boys.'

Four days later, the announcements in assembly included congratulations to Suzie Wilson on being awarded an exhibition to read history at Cambridge at Corpus Christi College. With bold determination, abandoning his customary fear of girls, Jimmy went up to Suzie in the prefects' room and quietly said,

'Excuse me, but I think you deserve a kiss', which he delivered full on the lips with no little passion.

When the couple married in the chapel at Corpus after graduating, they invited a few of their old school friends to be there. Janey Butler, now Janey Cooper, was delighted to attend with her husband, never having set foot in a university before. She told her man, 'Jimmy was never one for the girls until Suzie came along.'

A FEW FAVOURITE EXCERPTS

Rob Plant

The value of sparrows

For all who are ground down, or in an impenetrable fog:

A spark from nature ...

'Are not two sparrows sold for a penny? Yet not one of them will fall to the ground outside your Father's care. And even the very hairs of your head are all numbered. So do not be afraid; you are worth more than many sparrows.' – Matthew 10: 29–31 (NIV)

A loving memory ...

'From sinking sand He lifted me;
With tender hand He lifted me;
From shades of night to realms of light,
Oh, praise His name He lifted me!'

Charles H. Gabriel

Rob Plant

A foundation …

'With His feathers He will cover you, under His wings you will find safety. His truth is your shield and armour.' – Psalm 91:4 (ISV)

LAUGHING
(all the way to the Lubyanka)

Andrew Alexander

Back in the late 1960s, I made two trips to Russia. These were the days of the Cold War and well before the Union of Soviet Socialist Republics was finally broken up into Russia and its smaller satellite countries. Being of university age, coupled with the suspicions that our two countries had for each other, it took me ages to obtain the required travel visa, but get one I eventually did.

During my stay in Moscow I was assigned a guide or "minder", to make sure I was not "up to no good" or, perhaps even, to see if I was suitable to enlist as a "contact" on my return to England. Well of course my motives for the visit were entirely innocent and the delectable Natasha was great company and an excellent chaperone. At every state run hotel in which I stayed there was a redoubtable and fierce lady sitting at a desk on the floor leading to the various rooms. I had to check in with her, both when leaving or entering the room. And so the eye of the great Russian state was on me during the whole of the visit.

At that time the food was not great, other than the famous borsch soup which was mouth watering and really tasty. By contrast meanwhile, the people walked around largely looking worried and weighed down with the cares of life. I've not been back since and guess life has changed a great deal for people and hopefully for the better!

Anyway places such as Moscow, Leningrad, Tashkent, Minsk, Kiev and Alma Ata were wonderful places to visit with many varied and interesting sights. Sadly I found that Health & Safety was nothing then like what I imagine it is now and I vividly recall an internal flight from Tashkent to Kiev in the Russian State airline Aeroflot equivalent of a BAC 111. The flight was well oversubscribed so even as we gathered speed down the runway to take off several people (including one memorable lady carrying a bundle that turned out to be a baby) were quite simply standing in the aisle as if taking a ride on a bus. Presumably the rules have now been reviewed. Possibly.

As we rose into the sky a loud whooshing noise began, with the cabin filled by a cloudy misty substance and a really foul smell. This was definitely not smoke but was nonetheless extremely alarming. Like me the gentleman sitting next to me was not happy and was in white knuckle mode, gripping the armrest tightly. We were both much relieved when advised that all was OK and that there was just a small problem with the air conditioning system. The cabin soon cleared of the fumes and I was able to strike up conversation with my neighbouring passenger. He was, it turned out, a Belgian national and a teacher fluent in six languages. I struck up a firm friendship with Henri and over the years we would meet in London whilst I visited him at his home in Tournai Kain and he spent time with us here in Derby.

What an introduction.

GROWING OLD
IS NOT FOR SOFTIES

Peter Dawson

Getting on the first bus in the morning on which free passes may be used is like wading into the sea, with its bubbling silver surf that caps the waves. The population is growing old. You did know that, didn't you?

There are now more people in this country over sixty than under sixteen. One of the burdens today's young people are going to have to bear is that of increasing taxation required to meet the cost of state pensions for the elderly, and the funding of the NHS to pay for their health problems. An aging population is a costly feature of a welfare state.

The cost of keeping millions of old people alive is enormous. For many of us, it involves our being on a host of different medications. The present writer now has to take a tablet whose purpose is to stop all the others wrecking his insides. When the doctor first prescribed it, he smiled and shook his head on my asking if he was joking.

As old age creeps up on us, every day can be a tough proposition. Just getting out of bed in the morning can be a major engineering exercise. After eighty it is easy to become preoccupied with one's physical condition. Without our glasses, if we can find them, we can't see much. Everything takes much longer than before. Our hearing is unreliable; our hips and knees need surgery; our waterworks leak; our heart doesn't work as it once did and our blood clogs up the rest of the system.

As for our memory, we may have total recall when it comes to events in our lives many years ago but we can't remember what we were supposed to do yesterday. Mind you, when one's debility in that area is widely accepted, it can have its advantages. One elderly gent was heard to say, 'If I'd known I was going to live as long as this, I would have taken better care of myself.' Our extravagant carelessness about our physical life in our prime backfires on us in our later years.

We live at a time when much profit is to be had by helping people, and especially women, to stay looking young. The purveyors of cosmetics make amazing claims about removing the signs of age. For some women, notably those who are seen as celebrities, regular facelifts are the name of the game. One such has declared: 'I don't care if I have so many that my ears meet on top of my head.'

The avoidance of the signs of old age and approaching death is unsurprising in a society without belief in life after death. When the famous entertainer Roy Castle was dying of cancer he came across as a happy man, insisting that he was looking forward to what came next. He was very excited about it. Roy was a convinced Christian with great faith. Those of us who claim to believe the promises of Jesus ought to share Roy's attitude to popping our clogs.

RAMBLINGS

Corona Virus Dilemna

We are three weeks into self isolation and it is very upsetting for me to witness my wife standing at our living room window staring aimlessly into space with tears running down her cheeks. It breaks my heart to see her suffering like this and I have thought very hard how I can possibly cheer her up. I have even considered letting her in, but rules are rules.

Discretion and all that

I have learned that, in many situations, it is better to keep ones mouth firmly shut and let people think that you are a complete idiot than to open it and remove any vestige of doubt.

Ian Frearson

Memories

I never forget a face but with you I'll make an exception.

Groucho Marx

Observation on life

Sliding down this great bannister of life politics is just a splinter in your bottom.

Clever thoughts & quips

Everything should be kept as simple as possible – but not simpler.

Albert Einstein.

All that you know and all that you don't would fill a book

Charlotte Frearson

"We are all interested in the future because that is where you and I will spend the rest of our lives"
Criswell, announcer from the film 'Plan 9 from OuterSpace' voted "Worst film of all time"

Ramblings

Mr. Orvill (traveller to the Holy Land) "I want to walk where Jesus trod"
Herman Melville   "Where, on water?"

Je Suis Marxist – Tendence Groucho
                    On a Pissoire Wall in Paris